People buy things they need.

People use money to buy things.

Shopping

Around the World

Clare Lewis

Heinemann
LIBRARY
Chicago, Illinois

Edited by Joanna Issa, Shelly Lyons, Diyan Leake, and
Helen Cox Cannons
Designed by Cynthia Akiyoshi
Original illustrations © Capstone Global Library Ltd 2014
Picture research by Elizabeth Alexander and
Tracy Cummins
Production by Victoria Fitzgerald
Originated by Capstone Global Library Ltd

Library of Congress Cataloging-in-Publication Data
Lewis, Clare, 1976- author.
  Shopping around the world / Clare Lewis.
    pages cm.—(Around the world)
 Includes bibliographical references and index.
  ISBN 978-1-4846-0373-4 (hb)—ISBN 978-1-4846-
0380-2 (pb) 1. Shopping—Juvenile literature. 2. Popular
culture—Juvenile literature. I. Title.

TX335.5.L49 2015
381.1—dc23   2013040508

Image Crdits
Alamy: Jan Wlodarczyk, cover; Getty Images: Ali Trisno
Pranoto, 5, Image Source, 21, lillisphotography, 16,
MachineHeadz, 13, Michael Avina, 7, Michael DeYoung,
18, MoMo Productions, 9, 22 (bottom left), William
Andrew, 12, 23 (top); Shutterstock: AJP, 14, Brenda
Carson, 1, cosma, 24 (hat), GreenTree, 24 (cloth), Iakov
Filimonov, 17, back cover, Isabella Pfenninger, 2, Natali
Glado, 3, photostar72, 24 (car), revers, 24 (shoe), steve
estvanik, 19, ValeStoc, 8, Vladyslav Starozhylov, 24
(doll); SuperStock: agefotostock/Stefano Politi, 10, 22
(top left), 23 (bottom), Blend Images, 6, Ian Cumming/
Axiom - Design Pics, 11, imageBROKER/Egon Bömsch,
15, 22 (bottom middle), Nano Calvo/agefotostock, 20, 22
(top right), Robert Harding Picture Library/Michael Nola,
4, 22 (bottom right)

Every effort has been made to contact copyright holders
of material reproduced in this book. Any omissions will
be rectified in subsequent printings if notice is given to
the publisher.

Contents

Shopping Everywhere

All over the world, people
go shopping.

Different countries have different
money.

Where Do People Go Shopping?

People go to stores.
Some stores are big.

Some stores are small.

People go to markets.
Some markets are inside.

Some markets are outside.

Some people shop on the Internet.

The items are delivered to
their door.

What Do People Buy?

People go shopping to buy food.

People go shopping to buy clothes.

People go shopping to buy toys.

People go shopping to buy things
for their homes.

Getting the Items Home

Some people carry their items in bags.

Some people carry items on their heads.

Shopping is different all around the world.

Where do you go shopping?

Map of Shopping Around the World

Picture Glossary

Internet way of using computers that allows people who are far away to share information

market place where people buy and sell things. Many markets have small shops or stalls.

Index

Notes for parents and teachers

Before reading

Ask children about the last time they went shopping with someone. Where did they go? What did they buy? How did they pay for it? Show children the title and the contents page of this book. Read the entries and explain that the contents page is a tool to help readers know what information is in the book and where to find it. Ask children to predict what they will learn from this title after reading the contents page.

After reading

- Turn to page 12 and read the sentence. Ask children if they know what *Internet* means. Do any clues in the photograph help them know? Then turn to the glossary on page 23 and explain that a glossary is a tool that helps explain some of the more difficult words in the book. Find and read the definition for *Internet*.

- Point out the map on page 22 and demonstrate how to use the map to identify the continents on which different photos from the book were taken. Ask children where the photo on page 15 was taken (Morocco/Africa). Have children look at the details in the photo. What is being sold? Have they ever seen a market outdoors like this? What is similar and different between this market and where they go shopping?